T0137605

Reincarnation

Debbie Viale

AuthorHouse™
1663 Liberty Drive
Bloomington, IN 47403
www.authorhouse.com
Phone: 833-262-8899

Because of the dynamic nature of the Internet, any web addresses or links contained in this book may have changed
since publication and may no longer be valid. The views expressed in this work are solely those of the author and do
not necessarily reflect the views of the publisher, and the publisher hereby disclaims any responsibility for them.

Any people depicted in stock imagery provided by Getty Images are models,
and such images are being used for illustrative purposes only.
Certain stock imagery © Getty Images.

This book is printed on acid-free paper.

ISBN: 978-1-6655-4414-6 (sc)
ISBN: 978-1-6655-4416-0 (hc)
ISBN: 978-1-6655-4415-3 (e)

Print information available on the last page.

Published by AuthorHouse 11/26/2021

authorHOUSE®

Reincarnation

One day I walked for miles,
In hopes to find some peace,
The clouds were getting closer,
As I felt the raindrops hit my feet,
I slipped into a coffee shop,
And there is where I stayed,

Until the rain subsided,
And the sun came out again,
As I walked toward the door,
I felt myself being pulled back in,
So I looked around the room,
And this is what I found,

A man who looked a lot like you,
Who just sat and stared outside,
All of your expressions,
Were written on his face.
I asked him if we met before,
And this is what he said,

We were once man and wife,
Until I lost my life,
Then he showed me pictures,
And I began to cry,
How can I explain this vision,

Buried deep inside my soul,
I want to know more about him.
I thrive for answers too.
This man I thought I knew.
This man that looked like you.

You left so long ago,
That we never got the chance,
To finish what we started.
So this is what I said,
If you were my husband,
And I were your wife,

Then meet me where we married,
And we'll start a brand new life,
And that is where we met once more.
Before that dark, cold, rainy night,
Where my car went off the road,

And I vanished out of sight,
Now we dream together,
High up on a hill,
In hopes that our love lingers,
Like the children we instill….

Printed in the United States
by Baker & Taylor Publisher Services